I0555078

WAKE UP NOW!
——— IF A ———
MY BROTHERS
KEEPER
KEMI

WAKE UP NOW!
—— IF A ——
MY BROTHERS
KEEPER
KEMI

*God Promised Never
To Leave Us Alone*

PATRICIA PETER TAKANG

ARPress
ILLUMINATING IDEAS.
EMPOWERING VOICES

ARPress
45 Dan Road Suite 5
Canton MA 02021
Hotline: 1(888) 821-0229
Fax: 1(508) 545-7580

Ordering Information:
Quantity sales. Special discounts are available on quantity purchases by corporations, associations, and others. For details, contact the publisher at the address above.

Printed in the United States of America.

ISBN-13:   Paperback   979-8-89330-835-8
              eBook   979-8-89330-837-2
              Hardback   979-8-89330-836-5

Library of Congress Control Number: 2024902455

race and mercy be unto you, as Father God gives it freely. I was not only called; I was chosen. My whole life up until this very second has been orchestrated by my father god. If you are reading this book, it will guide you through your worst experiences and reveal what your duties are while here on planet earth: How to come above the evil acts of people being used to stop you and destroy you, how to talk to your angels of light , how to distinguish between good and evil acts, when to speak and when to be silent and when to fight. If you are an angel of light, then you are in a war with Father God at your side.

December 16,1950 is a day in infinity that a few knew would become the day of esoteric recognition. A black baby girl came to this universe so that all would have a chance to reunite with the Father and his angelic forces. Faith Bently was expected, but some people did not desire that she have a force within her that would set her above everyone except Father God. Family, friends, and neighbors recognized her gifts of the spirit before she walked. She walked after the age of three. She was tested by the unbelievers and feared by those who were also spiritually gifted but used their spiritual gifts negatively. Everybody desires to go to heaven, but no one wants to die. "Flesh cannot enter the kingdom of GOD".

"All have sinned and fallen shorts of the glory of GOD." You must truly understand these words. There are no pure human beings, only those whose falls have strengthened them whereby they have no desires to commit the same acts of sin. There are people who know they are committing evil acts but continue to act against Father God's will, and those who love Father God with all their hearts and souls. I was born on a cold winter night into a world that was beginning to embrace the love of money. Remember that the love of money was the root of all evil. I learned spiritually laws by observing people engaging in and practicing spiritual works. God did drop me in the proper environment. My family

1

and friends are highly spiritual people who taught me how to survive mental and physical abuse. Surviving under this environment is why I am successful. I not only have love for Father God also for his creation.

When I was very young, I lost my mother and father. I barely remember them; however, I remember scenes as though I was in a movie. I was with my grandmother on a trip from Donaldsonville New Orleans Louisiana. My grandmother explained that my grandfather was very sick and that she could not take care of us both. She talked to me about a lady's house we would visit on this trip. She explained that this lady would raise me; therefore, I would live with Shelley Mae, her two sons tommy and terry, and her common-law husband Ezekiel. We arrived at Shelley's home on Washington Avenue, and I met Tommy and Terry. Grandmother told me to get acquainted with the boys. Terry told me that he wanted to put my hat, coat, and gloves up for me and that he would return them when grandmother was ready to leave. Tommy was three years older than me a, and Terry was one year older than me. My grandmother was shouting at Shelley Mae because she declined to take me. When grandmother was ready to leave, I could not find my hat, coat, and gloves. Terry informed me that he had buried my things under the house. My grandmother admonished me for allowing the boys to bury my coat, hat, and gloves. I went under the house and removed the dirt off the lumps I saw. I left that house believing all the people living there were evil. I explained that to my grandmother, however, she was not concerned. She explained that my grandfather was very ill, and she could not take care of me and him. I was ready to leave my grandmother's house because she worked me so hard with washing clothes. I was very afraid that I would fall into the big tub of boiling water on a camp- like fire. I had to stir the clothes until they become clean. I always prayed that my guardian angels would prevent my fall. I believe I was six years old then. Grandmother would come out and squeeze the water out of the clothes and place them into another tub that she would fil with water to rinse the clothes. After Grandmother rinsed the clothes, I would hand her pins to hang the clothes on a clothesline. My father visited my grandmother's house and did not approve of me handling hot clothes. So, he called Shelley and she agreed to take me. I was told on my first day what was expected of me with the chores. Although Shelley took me into her house, she was not a loving mother to me.

I would watch Shelley Ann with her babies Rusty, Letty, and Esther. I would change their diapers, rinse the baby shit out of the diapers, and wash the diaper by hand every morning before going to school. Esther was born in February, and it was so cold in the winter, but I had to get the diapers clean before I went to school. Ezekiel had four nieces who lived with us when they had their babies in New Orleans at Charity Hospital. I had to wash their babies' diapers too. One morning, I started talking to my Father God. I asked why two of these females had anger for me instead of love. I started singing "Walk with Me Lord". While I am on my lonesome journey, I need you to walk with me. "I would sing to my Father God whenever the situation became overwhelming. One niece of Ezekiel treated me very well. She would make arrangements for me to wash the baby's diapers and she paid me. When she purchased fast-food, she would purchase the same for me. Her mother, one of Ezekiel's sisters, treated me differently than his other sisters. She displayed love to me and did not care who witnessed her love for me.

Shelly Mae gave me lessons that I did not have access to through anyone else. I took care of the elderly in my neighborhood. These people taught me lessons that re priceless until today. The boys I call brothers taught me to physically fight, and the elders taught me to spiritually fight. I enjoyed listening to wisdom. Shelley moved to the west bank of New Orleans, and I was happy. I transferred to my former high school but loved the people around me on the west bank of the river in Mississippi River. Shelley had many relatives on the west bank of the river in Algiers and Marrero (also known as Walker Town). When I was living in Uptown New Orleans, Shelley sent me to Walker Town to help her people with their dinner preparations on the weekend. These two sisters had what we call suppers. When someone publicized that they are "having a supper," everyone knew that these people would cook some special food to sell out of their home or bar. The food consisted of fried fish or deep-fried chicken with bake macaroni, potato salad, green peas, a slice of white bread, and a slice of cake. Gumbo would be favorite of everyone. I loved the two sisters and their children.

A young man, a friend of one of my cousins, asked me to walk with him to the store. He was to buy cigarettes for others shooting dices. He walked through Lincoln High School Stadium and attempted to rape me. I began to pray and ask Father God if this was necessary for me to serve him better. The young man got up and helped me to stand. He was surprised at my reaction to his attempted rape. We talked on the way back to my family's home. He told me that a family member whom I lived with in New Orleans paid him to kill me. When we returned to my cousins, all five men told this individual that he was luck he did not kill me. He asked how did you all knew, and one cousin replied we were asked first and refused. "We became worried because you took too long returning back with her," they said. They told me to go inside and get ready for bed. I followed their instructions.

The following evening, one of my make cousins who was younger than me - I was twelve years old at that time—tried to rape me, but I beat him with my fists. He pulled a straight razor out of his pocket, and I became angry. When I get angry, I literally see red. Everything disappeared and only red ran down a red wall. I don't remember anything but color red. My older male cousins informed me that I took the straight razor away from Conrad, lifted him into the air over my head, and threw him through the kitchen window. He got up from the ground and went to the bar to report my actions. He had a broken leg. His mother Merritt did not want to hear my side of the story; and the next day, she sent me home, back to Shelley Mae. I did not return until I was in my forties. They needed to know that I forgave them all. I was informed that Conrad kidnapped a nurse who was seeing a patient in his neighborhood, raped her several times, and kept her hostage. He was high on drugs and passed out. The nurse got free and ran down the street naked, screaming for help. Some neighbors called the police, and he was arrested and convicted to life prison. I believe that this event would not have happened if my family had believed me.

In 1966, Shelley Mae was working as a nurse's aide in a hospital on the west bank of the Mississippi. She brought home the largest apple I have ever seen and wanted me to eat it in her presence. My angels said, "No. Put it up for later." She told me that she got it from the hospital where she worked. There was a sixteen-year-old patient who had visited his people in Italy. He had contracted Diphtheria, a disease that was obliterated in United States. Shelley Mae was his nurse aide. She bathed him, change his bed linens. Emptied his trash can and delivered and removed his food tray from his room. She told us about this young man and that he may not survive this disease. Shelley Mae wanted to watch me eat this large apple. My angel said no, and I told Shelley Mae that I would eat it later. My younger brother Donald and younger sister Esther came to me the next day with the apple and cut it into three pieces. We each ate our portion and went out to play. Later that night, I left my body and saw my spirit floating over my body lying on bed. I was screaming because two angels were struggling to get me back into my body. I remember saying I don't want to return to that body; there is too much pain. Finally, the angels pulled me back into my body and I screamed so loud that I woke several neighbors. One of the neighbors called Shelley Mae at her job and told her to meet them at Charity Hospital Emergency Room. When we arrived at the hospital emergency room, the doctor came to me right away. I was asked what problem caused me to come to the emergency room at three in the morning. I opened my mouth to speak, but nothing came out. I pointed to the inside of my mouth to indicate a problem with my throat. The doctor sat down in front of me and asked to open as wide as I could. When he turned on the flashlight, he fell off his chair to the floor. He immediately got up and ran from the examination room to get other doctors to come and see. The head doctor looked into my mouth, and he ran from the room and ordered a quarantine of all staff members working in the hospital and all employees who worked in the emergency room or who had been there after I arrived. I was immediately admitted to contagious building. Doctors who specialize in infectious diseases were called in from other states. The next day, my brother Donald and sister Esther were admitted too. We were in the same room. A friend's sister was admitted and placed in the room with us. However, several hours later, she was removed. She appeared to be sleeping. Later, a nurse informed me that she had died. This little girl was about nine years old, and she was a twin. Her twin sister was not infected with diphtheria. I grieved her passing because she received it because she drank a cola behind me. Her brother and I were friends; he saw me at a school dance the night before I, my sister and brother were admitted to the hospital because of this disease. My throat was burning, and I felt like something was stuck in it. I explained to the doctor that I was miserable all day because of this. A doctor from another country who had much experience with diphtheria was called to come examine me at Charity Hospital in New Orleans. The specialist doctors had questioned us, but until twin died, I had not made the connection to the apple and twin drinking from a soda I gave to her brother because my throat really hurt when I took a sip. I requested to speak to the head doctor, and I explained to him what connected all of us. The doctor told me that they knew that I was virgin; however, a kiss could cause the infection. This disease was highly contagious, and someone drinking or eating from a person with this disease will definitely become infected with diphtheria. Shelley had informed the doctor that the twin's brother was my boyfriend. They thought that the twin may have drunk her brother's cup. But the brother was not infected. He had same conclusion for my sister and brother: that they both drank my cup; that was not true. The head doctor informed me that Shelley Mae said to them, "Faith Pierre don't know anything, let me talk to the doctors for her" I told this doctor of the situation whereby Shelley Mae brought a very large red apple from her job for me. I was afraid to eat the apple because Shelley Mae was not kind to me. Out of the seven children living at her house. I was the only one not given anything special, not even a hug. I explained to the doctor that the sixteen-year-old boy who was contagious first with diphtheria, nurse's aide at a hospital in Algeria, was Shelley Mae. She was responsible for bathing him, hanging his sheets, taking his vitals, bringing him his food tray and retrieving the tray after he had eaten. The doctor called the hospital where she worked and confirmed what I told them to be the truth. This doctor called the New Orleans Police department and asked them to pick her up and bring h her to him in Charity Hospital. I could hear this doctor threatening her with jail time if she did not tell him the truth. He accused her of starting an epidemic in her family, the hospital staff, and her community. She confessed that she gave that apple after inserting a needle found in the patient's trash can. The next day, my brother and sister were discharged from the hospital. No, Shelley Mae was not arrested because she was promised that if she told the truth, she would not be arrested. The head doctor and the specialist doctors visited me every day. They were concerned that Shelley Mae might be successful in trying to kill me. They asked me if I knew why she wanted me dead and congratulated me on being intelligent enough to help them solve the problem. Several events have happened to me before the diphtheria-injected apple. I told them about another incident where I was poisoned by Shelley Mae's oldest son Tommy Pierre. He forced me and my brother Donald to drink sulfur mixed into water. I was not affected because I drank very little; however, my brother drank a lot and had to be rushed to Charity Hospital Emergency room. What saved us was Shelley's aunt living with us that time. Her name was Beth Nash. We called her Aunt Tea. Aunt Tea was blind and an elderly person, meaning old. She may have been in her seventies or eighties. She was very spiritual and could see something happening before it happened. She could also see people who had passed from this sphere to another. Aunt Tea had the gift of prophecy, healing, discernment, and many more. Ministers would visit her daily to receive prayers and healing. When she came to live with Shelly Mae, my brother Donald and I fell in love with her. Aunt Tea asked Shelly Mae to allow me to take care of her while Shelly went to work, her club meetings, and parties, which happened every weekend. She taught me how to survive. Aunt Tea and I prayed for Donald every day because he wanted Shelly Mae's two oldest boys to love him. He was beaten up every day. I had to fight for him every day, and every day, I got beaten up until I threaten death by any means necessary. When Aunt Tea realized what was happening, she called Donald and me to her bedside where she sat in a rocking chair and prophesied to each of us who we are in God's house. Donald did not want the life she described to him because he would have few friends. However, I was very happy to know that Father God had chosen me for something great. Aunt Tea called the police to come get Donald and bring him to Charity Hospital when he drank the poison that was meant for me. I tried to get Donald to vomit, but he run from me, and I had to throw up myself. When I was eight and Donald was seven years old, we were playing hide-and-seek with Tommy and Terry. Donald was instructed to hide with me in some bushes on the corner of our house. The day before, I witnessed Tommy and Terry throw their dead dog there after it was hit by a train. Donald pulled me to the corner and tried to get me in the bushes, but I told him that the dog was there dead. He jumped right on the dog's teeth and had to receive several stitches and rabies shots. I believe to this day that Aunt Tea's spiritual lessons are the reason I lived to complete my Father God Mission. Shelly Mae complained to the other family members that Aunt Tea was causing problems among her children. Ms. Jameson, Shelly Mae's oldest cousin, took Aunt Tea to live with her. Donald and I would sneak to see Aunt Tea while Ms. Jameson was at work. We would climb up Aunt Tea's bedroom window and give her water and food we took from home. Some days, I would not eat breakfast and take it to Aunt Tea before I went to school. One day when we visited Aunt Tea, she instructed Donald and me to stop visiting her. She stated that she heard Ms. Jameson and a neighbor scheming to call the police when Donald comes into her home again without her permission. Aunt Tea held Donald and me and told us, "Goodbye. Don't come back." It felt a knife was being twisted in my heart. When I considered her brown eyes, I knew I would not see her again—that she was going to Father God very soon. I cried because she was the one person I loved so much that I believed I could not live without her presence. One week later, she was dead. On another occasion, I was sent to live with Shelly Mae's cousin Amelia Walker in Walkertown on the west bank for the summer. Walkertown is now known as Marrero. I was eleven years old, and my cousin pulled a straight razor out of his pocket and told me to lie down on his bed. I refused and he informed me that he was told to cut my throat in the woods. He said that he wanted sex from me first. I took the blade after he sliced my upper right leg and threw him through his mother's window. He ran to the bar where they hung out at night and told them that I threw him through the window. One of the adults drove me home to Shelly Mae the following day, I returned to see Shelly Mae's cousin when I was thirty-two just to show forgiveness and love.

My life change after the diphtheria-injected apple. I looked for someone to take me from Shelly Mae's house. I met Larry a year the diphtheria-injected apple. A year later, we were married. I believed God sent me this man because we were married in predominately white Catholic Church in Jefferson Parish on the west bank of the river. We were given the High Mass Wedding Ceremony. The Catholic Church has mandatory counseling for their engaged couples. Larry was Catholic, but I wasn't.

the priest thought that I was Catholic because I attended his church every Sunday. The counseling sessions were held three months.

There were six couples including Larry and Me. The couples enjoyed my jokes and ability to be relaxed and loving toward them. Remember this occurred in the late 60's when it was rare to see blacks and whites acting friendly toward each other. Our last meeting found Larry and I being offered in the High Noon Wedding Mass. We accepted the offer. We consent it with the priest, and I was very happy. On our wedding day, we discovered that the other couples decided to leave their decorations for our wedding. There were two weddings scheduled before our wedding and two scheduled after our wedding, and all their decorations were placed for our wedding. I cried because that was the first time a stranger gave me something without asking for something in return.

Larry married Faith Pierre on April 20, 1968. The wedding was held at Saint Juliana Amor Catholic Church on the west bank of New Orleans. Everyone kin to me appeared for this wedding. Shelly Mae was busy she almost missed me cutting my cake. The reception hall people were there to start cleaning up, and she had left with a carload of people. I encouraged these people to wait. She returned five minutes later, and we cut our cake. We took pictures and went home.

Our home was a house shared with Larry's older sister, her husband, and their two-year-old son. Our bedroom was the first room you would enter outside. Everyone who came to visit had to walk through our bedroom. These were the happiest days of my Life; however, this was only the beginning of lessons I needed to be successful.

In July, I had a miscarriage, and it was a boy. Two months later, Larry and I moved to a one bedroom double. Cynthia her husband, Sam Sr., and their two-year-old moved to the other side of the double. I babysat Sam Jr., Cynthia, and Sam's baby boy, while they worked. In December 1968, I became pregnant. How do I know this? I knew each time I became pregnant I was sure because I received an electrical current pass through the pelvic area of my body. I carried this child for nine months without any problems. However, we moved out of this house before Arthur's birth because it was haunted. I can see spirits or ghosts and I witnessed two little white children aged four and five. They would run through the house laughing and hiding from each other. My two-year-old nephew Sam Jr. and I would eat our breakfast out on the porch because I thought he was scared of spirits. His father Sam Sr. (Cynthia's Husband) told me that he heard them running through our house every morning, and so he talked to Cynthia about moving. I told Larry that I wanted to move, but Larry did not want to leave Cynthia, his sister, in this house. Larry, myself, Sam, and Cynthia had a meeting several nights later and we all decided to move back to the seventh ward. This house was located in the sixth ward of New Orleans. The City of New Orleans is, unto this day, divided by ethnicity. We were living in Italian section of New Orleans, and we moved to the Creole or French section of New Orleans. When my first living son was six months old, Shelly Mae purchased a 235 HUD home. It was located twenty-five miles from New Orleans. I was visiting her when my second son, Josiah, was born in September 1970. We moved to a one-bedroom house where my husband worked across the street shucking oysters. Larry's aunt, his father's sister, and her family lived one house down the street. We lived there for one year, and my offer for a one bedroom located in the Iberville Project came through. We moved there, and my fourth pregnancy occurred. I was fighting with my husband because he partied for two days without checking on me. This pregnancy expired when he left the following morning for work. The doctors at Charity Hospital in New Orleans informed me that the baby had not developed and that is why I miscarried the infant. That happened in 1971. The Iberville Development projects gave me a two-bedroom apartment. I was pregnant again and I just knew this was a girl. I had a problem with my digestion system. Everything I ate become a problem. Levi was born July 1972 and I thought, *That's enough*. Three boys. However, I wanted a girl so my fourth son, Mark, was born in September 1973 and my fifth son Raphael in September 1974.

The following years were great. I raised my sons and was a volunteer in their first-grade classes. I attended a training school for welding because my husband Larry needed help with the bills. I didn't finish because he claimed that I was around too many men who also attended this training. The school was one block from Xavier University, and for my one-hour period. I went to Xavier University and inquired about attending classes there. I was informed that I needed to obtain my high school diploma. I talked to my husband concerning this matter, and he agreed that I should do whatever it took to obtain my diploma. The next month after I graduated from welding class, I placed an application with Urban League Street Academy. That was where I met Ms. Mary Galleon, and she fell in love with my five boys. I was there for less than a year and graduated third in my class. My friends Camila Lewison and Lester Thomas, who also attended Urban League Street Academy.

Graduated with me. Both majored in business administration and is majored in medical technology. In my second year there, the University dropped medical technology; therefore, I changed my major to physics. Physics was great for me; however, I was spending too much time at the library with my sons in tow. Larry needed me to work, so I quit school.

My husband started complaining about needing more money to manage our family. The State of Louisiana placed an ad in the local newspaper the *Times Picayune* for jobs with that state prison and the Army National Guard. I also applied with City Bus but declined it to work for the State of Louisiana. The state prison system was preparing a Work Training Facility-South to operate through the National Guard. However, they wanted civilians as employees for this operation.

I scored a 99 on the test I was given, and the board I met with for an interview was delighted. I was hired and I began training the following Monday at the Work Training Facility-South on Delery Street in New Orleans. This was also known as Jackson Barracks before it became Work Training Facility-South. This site was a mental facility for the criminally insane prisoners. These individuals were transferred out over a period, and I got to understand what happened to them while they were there. I trained with the National Guard, watching prisoners at the National Guard Facility cutting grass, cleaning the area, cooking, and working under some of the soldiers.

The state police picked up the inmates who worked at their site. I was the first woman to work one-on-one with the male prisoners under Angola. When I was hired, Mr. Putnam was the warden and he had been excommunicated from the Catholic Church. My family was Catholic, and I did not know how to interact with him. I was fired three times because I taught the inmates to write. Yes, there was an individual who taught classes there once a month. What the people did not understand was that at least 80 percent of black men from my neighborhood were there.

When I look back over my life and analyze what happened and why it happened, I see and understand that these actions and decisions help me mold me for what I had to do. I understand that the men I knew from my neighborhood were my brothers. These men also knew me that I could not be a friend while working at the prison. I graduated from nursing school, and after the third time I was fired, I went to work as a licensed practical nurse. I never returned to work there; however, I did clear my name and I resigned from Work Training Facility-South. Although I could not understand at the time why I went through these lessons, I absolutely understand now. I can say that this job taught me everything I needed to be successful in my life: understanding and communicating with people. I hope that through my experiences you will understand your plight also.

My sons were great at watching each other while I worked, or so I thought. One day, I was working in the morning shift during summer break and had to come home early after receiving a call from an elderly neighbor. My elderly neighbor met me at my car and asked me to follow her inside her home. She explained to me that my children had girls in my house while I was at work. These girls have run away from home and are living with an older man around the corner from our house. I grew up in the 50's-60's, and our neighbors were our family too. If a neighbor told you to stop playing and go inside until your parents returned home, you must obey. If a child did not obey, he/she could bet and win that the neighbor will physically beat that child, and when Mom or Dad returned home, they would surely be beaten and punished. On this occasion, I went into the house, and all my children were looking at the television in the family room. I had no evidence; therefore, I said nothing about the girls being in my home while I was at work. To cover up his sexual acts while I was working and taking classes, my oldest son had a friend of his girlfriend attempt having sex with the other four boys, his brothers. His understanding was if they did what he did, then no one could rat him out. Well, my oldest son came to and confessed what he had been doing for a month.

He stated that he could not urinate because of burning sensation in his penis. I took him and my second son, whom my first son swore had sex with the same girl he had sex with, to Delgado Clinic. My second son denied having sex with the young lady and told me that he faked it to get his brother off his time about sex. My second son Josiah, reported that the girl told him she had an STD. I insisted that he come to Delgado Clinic with his oldest brother and myself. He did, and his test was negative. However, his big brother's test positive, and he was shocked that this girl gave him this disease. He was given two antibiotic's to take, and was ordered not to have sex until he returned to the clinic. He was also surprised that his brother faked having sex with the same girl. Josiah smiled all the way home.

My five sons and I have many life experiences we can look back upon and understand and that those lessons were intended to teach and strengthen us for future events in our life. I know that communication is one of the greatest gifts God has given us. My son's and I went to Disney in Florida several times. I appreciate my boy's interactions and when we traveled to Disney Land in Florida, it was a treat for me too. I volunteered at St. Levi's University after my bachelor's degrees. Three sons graduated from St. Levi's University with bachelor's degree. These experiences united my family. This united our family, and my boys entertained me by inviting their friends to get their high school diploma through me as a proctor working for St. Levi's University. Two sons wanted to drive tractor trailer trucks. I found a company close to my house in New Orleans. Both sons applied and attended to the classes and graduated with my finances. Did anyone pay me back? No. However, I did receive thank you from their mothers. I actually raised these boys while their mothers went work or was a party woman. My children had their friends at my house every day. They ate there and played there. Yes, my food bill was very high. When my oldest boy became a teenager, I was content to work one job. This gave me more time to be with my children. My five boys were different in many ways. I engaged them in our local park's little league football team. Our neighborhood had more boys than girls. The girls did not play with the boys. My house was the place to hang out. I learned why black boys behave the way they do. I grew up with boys because I had four brothers who lived with me in the same house for twelve months out the year until I got married, and one stepbrother lived with us during the summer months.

I remember that my childhood was very different from my brother's. I would walk three blocks to St. Charles Ave. where old money resided. I was permitted to explore my community and my wealthy neighbors embraced me, but my brothers would be beaten and arrested if they survived the beating for merely walking in that community.

Grace and Mercy be unto you as Father GOD gives it freely. I was not only called but I was chosen. My whole life up until this very second has been orchestrated by my Father God. If you are reading this book, it will guide you through your worst experiences and reveal what your duties are while here on Planet Earth. How to come above the evil acts of people being used to destroy you. How to talk to your Angels of Light. How to distinguish between Good and Evil acts. When to speak and when to be silent and when to fight. If you are an angel of light when to go to war for Father God.

THE SEASON OF AWAKENING IS NOW

Are You Awakening?

I am now classified as not just the Father's daughter but an undeniable soldier for our Father God. When you are called by Father God, you will know. Keep the faith; this battle is difficult and lonely. Potential friends turn out to be the worst enemies. If you have ears, hear me. If you have vocal cords, speak. If you have a heart, show it by standing and fighting for Father God. Doing the Father's will, will determine if you would be successful. I have been vocal for my Father God all my life. Have I paid for serving him? Yes. I will serve him until I am physically, mentally, spiritually, and emotionally finished in this body, whereby whatever form I take will continue to serve Him.

Three sons joined the United States Navy. Actually, my second son Josiah Sr. influenced his oldest brother Arthur Sr. and his youngest brother Jose Sr. to follow him into the US Navy. He worked in the mail room, and today he has his own trucking company. My oldest son was a cook on the ship *USS New Orleans*. His captain was a New Orleans native. What a coincidence. Today he has his own trucking company. My youngest son Jose was accepted to train in the navy nuclear program where he reenlisted for four more years.

He stayed on the ship eight years before obtaining his honorable discharge. He got married and had three boys before discharging from the navy. His training helped him to obtain a job at a nuclear power plant. He is now the training officer after being on this job for fifteen years. My third son, Levi Sr., graduated from St. Levi's University. He works across the United States with Bros Brothers, and he also drives tractor trailer truck. My fourth son, Mark, also graduated from St. Levi's University obtaining his GED. He was a natural repairman for electronics. He worked for major cable companies where he ran cable throughout the residents and major lines from the poles to the houses. Decades later, he would wire the new Veteran Administration Hospital and the newly built LSU Hospital for cable. Mark did not attend school above the high school level. He taught me to never give up. Because this son was a difficult child. If you said to him "don't do it," he did it. God promised never to leave me alone. Miguel got married and fathered two girls and two boys.

Archangel Michael spoke to me as I awakened from a good night's sleep. He informed me to prepare my bedroom for a visit from him. I stripped the walls of the sheet rock and sanded the wall until most of the green paint was removed. The walls were pine, and the aromatic smell of pine is very nice. I washed the walls down and waited two days for the wood to completely dry. I painted the walls with two applications of stain and allowed them to dry for one day. The following day, I applied two applications of polyurethane to the wood walls and allowed one day to dry. The bed was not removed from my bedroom as I remodeled the room. Levi Sr. helped me change the blades of my ceiling fan from dark brown to pine. The room was very calming, and I enjoyed just being there.

Levi Sr. was the only son living with me, and his two-year-old son visits me at least four days a week. Levi Sr. had his son Levi Jr. with him and decided to have a sleepover at my house. I cooked dinner and we ate, and I and my grandson Levin Jr. retired to my bedroom. When I entered the bedroom with Levi Jr. in my arms, he threw his body back and his eyes rolled back in his head. I was only three feet into the bedroom, so I backed out. Levi Jr. looked into my eyes, and it was clear to me that he was not having convulsions. I walked back to the family room and instructed his father to bring him home. I explained to Levi Sr. that something was going to happen in my bedroom before daybreak and his son would not survive the event. Levi Sr. walked his son back into my bedroom and his head went back and his eyes rolled back into his head. Levi Sr. knew then that I was on to something, so he drove his son Levi Jr. to grandmother's house. I took a bath and retired to my rocking chair and the Bible. Josiah was discharged from the navy three days before this event, and he accompanied his brother to bring Levi Jr. home,

When they returned home, they went to their bedroom. I had spiritual music playing in my bedroom, and I fell asleep around eleven thirty. I woke up in the rocking chair and looked at the clock; it was three in the morning. I spread a blanket over my bed. This blanket was purchased in Jerusalem by my oldest son Arthur Sr. when the *USS New Orleans* was there for a few months. He was informed by the merchant that the blanket would save his mother's life. This was the first time I placed the blanket on my bed because it was summer. I was in the bed for approximately three minutes when my bedroom door to the front porch flew open. There stood several teenagers, one of whom kicked my door in but remained standing on my front porch. One of the youths had tears rolling down his cheeks. I thought, *I don't recognize any of these youths.* I had a premonition that something was going to happened to me for several days. Archangel Michael appeared between me and the youths who were holding machine guns. He appeared to be too tall for my ceiling, but I could see all of him. Archangel Michael commanded me to pull the blanket over my entire body and roll out of bed. I replied to Archangel Michael that I intended to run from this room into my son's bedroom. Everything went into slow motion at that point while God's angel informed me that I am here in this state of being because I tell God what I am going to do and refuse to follow orders from God's angels. As long as I can remember, I've had interactions with angels. But I was not aware that I was acting like a spoiled child until God's angel spoke it to me. I did not talk back. I immediately rolled out of the bed wrapped in the spiritual blanket decorated with Jesus attending to children. As I turned my body toward the floor, I felt the first bullet hit directly over my aorta and the next three bullets into my right arm. I lay on my bedroom floor praying that my two sons would survive this. When I removed the blanket from my face, the boys with the machine guns were gone. My sons run into my room and ask me if I was OK. Levi Sr. asked me if I was shot. I replied that the first bullet hit me in my chest, but my right side and right under arm was burning. Josiah called the police, and they came fifteen minutes later although the Fifth District Police Station was located five blocks from my house. These policemen knew me because I worked at Jackson Barracks under the state police and with the Army National Guard Military Police as a federal police officer. The ambulance attendants were allowed into my house, and they staged a scene where everyone out in the street would believe that

I was dead. I was taken out on a stretcher with the sheet covering my entire body. I was instructed not to move. My two sons followed the ambulance to Charity Hospital where the doctors examined me and took x-rays to find the bullets. I explained that I was a nurse and asked one of my sons to hold the bullets until they asked for them. I told the doctors to call both sons into my room. Josiah gave the doctor the bullets and informed the doctors that at least forty bullets were in the walls in my bedroom. The doctor informed us that there was no need for surgery because all the bullets passed through my body and did not injure any organs, veins, or arteries. He instructed me that I could go home tomorrow. The doctor came to see me the following morning and informed me that the hospital security watched me all night. I knew everyone in the security staff because I escorted prisoners from Jackson Barracks to Charity Hospital Clinics. The hospital security staff would give me two fifteen-minute breaks when I had to stay with the inmates in the clinics when they were admitted to the hospital. My brother Donald and Shelly Mae came to the hospital to bring me home. Donald had a caliber .45 gun he proudly showed me. Donald informed me that he would be sleeping on my bedroom floor, next to my bed. He explained that the gun would be cocked in his hand just in case the youths came back to finish the job. I was more concerned about getting shot by him instead of the youths. Donald had seizures, and I could see him having a seizure with this gun cocked while he was lying on the floor next to me in bed. I was shocked and surprised at his plan to protect me but convinced him that I would not sleep with him in my house with a cocked gun. I spoke calmly, and I was very precise. Just as Shelly Mae parked in front of my house, Donald decided to give her the gun. I went inside, and my neighbors came to encourage me that the community is investigating, and they have some solid information. I prayed when they left my home. The young men who sat on my front porch and back porch would not leave. They were childhood friends, state policemen and city policemen visiting me while I recuperated. My family and friends decided to have a family meeting. I was informed that the boys involved in my shooting lived around the corner from us and had recently moved there. The story was that this family was evicted from Desire Project. This family was headed by their grandmother because someone shot and killed their mother years ago. This woman came to my house the next day and apologized for her grandson's actions. She informed me that I was shot because one of sons hit three of the boy's mother and her grandson was friends with them. She added that her grandson turned himself in and she will not bail him out because she was afraid that my son's friends would kill him. I promised her not to worry because I would talk to everyone. My son Levi Sr. went to talk to this woman and her three sons also turned themselves in. A court date was set, and my family attended. The boys claimed that they did not know anyone else connected to the crime and informed the court that they were not guilty. The judge set a trial date for one week later. My oldest son walked past the defendant's table while the judge talked to their attorney.

I don't know what he said, or if he even said a word. He came and sat next to me. All three boys raised their hands, verbally declaring their guilt. The judge asked their attorney if they were guilty or not guilty. Their attorney said not guilty, and the three boys said, "We want to fire this attorney and throw ourselves before the mercy of the court. We are guilty, Your Honor." The judge asked me to stand, and he apologized to me. He said that the boys' counsel convinced him that these boys were innocent. He told me that I could speak to the court now. I spoke and looked all the three boys in their eyes. I asked them if they knew me, and all the three said no. I stated that the only reason I am living at this time is Father God. I explained that my mission is to save young black males from prison by bringing them to Africa. I said, "If you can experience Africa, your life will change. I believe that Satan used all of you to stop me and you did your best. God the Father said no." I showed the court the x-rays where I was shot and how the bullets entered my body and came out under my right arm. I pointed to the wound above my aorta where the bullet made an S and exited just below my arm pit. Then I turned to the judge and asked him to sentence them to a work training facility, just not Work Training Facility-South. The judge asked me how I knew about Work Training Facility-South. I replied that I was the first female correctional officer to work there. I informed him that I helped in building this program after the psychic unit was transferred out.

The judge was appalled that the counsel for the defendants did not inform the court that the plaintiff was a law enforcement officer. The judge dismissed their attorney and asked his clerk to set a date for the sentencing of the defendants and for the defendants' lawyer to meet with him later during the week. The judge told me he was very happy that I survived this ordeal. He informed me that I don't have to return for their sentence date. He thanked me for my information. The judge asked the three youths to stand and apologize to me.

They did apologize to me, and they also asked their mother to forgive them. They asked the judge to keep them there until sentencing. The judge obliged and asked the sheriff to return them to their cells. My sons, the defendants' mother, and myself walked out of the court together, and she apologized to me. She informed me that my son Levi Sr. slapped her in the presence of her sons. She told her sons that she hit him first and she thought everything was ok but it wasn't. I hugged this mother and let her know that no one will touch her sons. I asked her to move out of the neighborhood because the twenty-one-year-old man who convinced her sons to shoot me was hiding and may hurt her because her sons gave the judge his name.

My son Arthur Sr. informed the boys' mother that everyone was in trouble if the judge's opinion was different. I asked Arthur Sr. to return to his navy base in San Diego, California, and I purchased the ticket. He left very early in the next morning.

A very good friend of mine asked me to buy a house he remodeled just three houses down from my house. He sold me his house for $9,000. There wasn't any work needed. My grandson Arthur Jr. moved in with me because of a court order giving my son, Arthur Sr., and me custody. We were very comfortable and not looking to leave the neighborhood. A storm named Georges moved into the Gulf of Mexico and sat at the mouth of the Mississippi River for several days. The effect to us was that our roof redone, and the first and second bedrooms had to be totally remodeled. I completed all the interior work myself. A roofer actually applied asbestos tiles back on the roof. The city asked me to move because my new roof was asbestos, and Arthur Jr. became ill because of the asbestos. Because the move was an emergency move, Housing Authority of New Orleans paid my rent. Before my first grandson and

I moved to the West Bank of New Orleans, I obtained sainthood under Shango and Yameya through the Cubans. I was informed that my talents would be used differently from others who received Orisha. It was because I received all the Orisha. Prophecy given at the ceremonies in Miami, Florida, took place over a two-week period.

I was blessed by a Babaloua from Nigeria, Africa. Arthur Jr. did not attend these ceremonies, but upon my return from Florida, he was spiritually reviewed, and the determinations were that Ogun and Oshun were his head angels. He received his warriors and continued to grow spiritually. I dated a Cuban Babaloua for several months. This baba loved my grandson, Levi Jr., and he gave him his warriors.

I learned much through him; however, he was not to be in my future. He prepared me for my African spiritual journey. I was informed that this man of God returned to Cuba where he died in an automobile accident.

I met Victoria Seeker just after these events. Victoria informed me that she was kin to me. I invited her to my house and introduced her to Shelly Mae, who had been convincing me for decades that she was my biological mother. Shelly Mae was living next door to me because I purchased the house next door for her. Shelly Mae recognized Victoria and stared, "You are Lucite's daughter!" Victoria answered, "Yes, I am. And we are taking Patricia back." Shelly Mae went into her house slamming the door, and decided to move back to Hammond, Louisiana, the next day.

Victoria returned to my home the next day and asked me to come and visit her where she worked. My oldest son, Arthur Sr., accompanied me. She worked in a botanica as a spiritual reader. She informed me that I would be in Africa in December 2005 where I would receive and IFA.

We moved into an apartment on the west bank. Emmanuel, my prophet, had given me a reading in 1995 that was my calling, and I recalled that he wanted me to prepare to go on my life mission to Africa. Emmanuel and my mother died in 1995 after my spiritual ceremony which took place in June 1995. My brother Donald Pierre had informed me years earlier how to prepare to travel to Africa. He was an accountant for the First National Bank of Chicago and was assigned in Nigeria, Africa, over a ten-year period. Donald returned to America due to my mother's death, and he was on workman's comp. He died in November 1996. When Donald went into the hospital, he called me to repot that he had papers he received from Shelly Mae. He explained that the papers would lead me to money left by older people in the family to fund my mission. I asked Donald to give me the information. He informed me that I had a bank account with Whitney Bank. The money generated interest over a fifty-year period, and family members have assets to obtain the interest. He asked me to be careful. I went to the Whitney Bank the next day, and the president was not surprised to see me. However, he informed me that he and my brother were correcting the account on my behalf. I left the bank facing a vacation, my sister Vicky Pierre, brother Tommy Pierre and Donald's wife Bertha Pierre from Nigeria, Africa, visited Donald while he was in the hospital's intensive care unit (ICU). He was there because someone had poisoned him, but he recovered. His doctor was concerned that too many people were in the waiting room waiting to visit him. He was concerned because Donald had the doctor place a no visitor sign in his chart. When the doctor left the hospital heading home, he received a call from the ICU informing him that his patient was having seizures and vomiting blood. He was thirty minutes from the hospital, and he returned as fast as he could. When he entered the ICU, the emergency room doctor in charge had pronounced Donald dead. My sister Esther called me and left a message to go to the hospital and stop my sister and brothers from killing Donald. I returned home several hours after Donald was pronounced dead. I did not receive the message until the following day because my brother Terry had been to my house and disconnected my phone. He loosened the flexible gas pipe, which I discovered when I walked into my kitchen. How did I know it was Terry? My neighbors saw him go under my house, and he had a key to the house. As far as I can remember, I could smell gas when no one else could smell gas. I called a friend and asked him to come and tighten my flexible gas pipe to the main pipe. He arrived and immediately observed the problem. He asked me if I had loosened the pipe more. I informed him that I did not touch the flexible pipe. He explained to me that the two pipes were not connected at all. He asked me not to allow my brother Terry back into my house. I forgot to ask him to check my phone wires under the house. My son Josiah came later, and he discovered the phone wires under my house were not connected. He connected the wires, and I immediately could use my phone. Now I have witnesses that could back my accusations that my brother Terry was attempting to kill me. Josiah begged me not to go to his uncle Terry's house. Terry asked me to come and spend a week or two at his house because mother had died in the hospital, and he missed her. He convinced me that I looked just like her and this would calm him. Arthur and I talked about this situation, and we agreed to stay with him for one week. My third night at Terry's house was disturbing to me. I fell asleep reading the bible with six-year-old Arthur Jr. next to me in bed. All my Orisha were in the closet in my room. I was in mother's hospital room, and Terry entered the hospital room. He walked past me and lay across her hospital bed. She spoke to him and said, "I am very tired" because Daddy Perry and other ancestors were interfering with her sleep. He did not move off the bed but instead places his body on top of her body. She said, "Get off of me now. I cannot breathe." Then I realized that his right forearm was under her chin, pressing her neck. He pushed up on his toes, forcing his weight into her neck. I then shouted, "Kick him in the groins!" But she faintly repeated, "Terry stop… Terry, stop… Terry, stop" and attempted to push him off of her. And I heard her voice saying, "Sister, wake up! Terry is here in your room to kill you. He heard you telling me to kick him in the groins! Wake up now!" u jumped in the middle of the bed. Terry was holding a large butcher knife. He immediately hid it behind his back, but it was too late because I saw the knife. I ordered him out of my room, and he responded that I was at his house, and he didn't have to leave. I ordered him to leave the house until I get all of my stuff out. He ordered me to tell him what his mother said to me since her death. I replied that he did not believe in life after death. He agreed and walked out of the house, entered his car, and left. Arthur Jr. slept through it all. I woke Arthur Jr. up and informed him that we had to leave quickly. We placed all my clothes, Arthur's school clothes, and my Orisha in my trunk. As we left Terry's apartment, a neighbor asked if we were all right. I thanked her for her concern and left. Arthur Jr. and I went back to our home on Derbigny Street. Two days later, Arthur Jr. went to stay with his uncle Josiah while I went to the Florida shores.

My Baba prayed for me, and I prayed for my mother's soul. Donald was not in the hospital when I left, but Donald died in the hospital before I could return.

When I arrived at the church where Donald's body was, there was an elderly black woman sitting in the middle of the church. I arrived early to perform a cleansing for the dead on him. My friend Katrina was with me, and she sat with the elderly woman while I prayed. He had a frown on his face when we first enter the church but when I completed the prayers, he had a smile on his face. The elderly woman and Katrina approached the casket when I motioned for them to come and see. The elderly woman thanked me with a hug and left. Katrina and I sat on the first row and watched family members arrive. I have never attended a funeral where the immediate family are not sitting in front of the body. Donald's wife, Tommy's wife, and I were the only family members sitting in front. I was allowed to speak at Donald's funeral, but I had to stop because I realized that he directed me to my spiritual mission, and he died for me. We were thick as thieves, white on rice, and I miss him very much. I thank God daily for his mission. I haven't received my inheritance, but when I do, I will remember his children financially.

I went to the coroner's office to talk to the coroner concerning Donald's death. I was surprised that he knew Donald. Donald was a sheriff and a minister, and he counseled inmates in Hammond, Louisiana Jail. He informed me that Donald was concerned for my safety with our brother Terry. Donald's doctor called him and informed him that he had spoken to me, Donald's oldest sister. He informed the coroner that Donald had given him information that his family should not visit him. He was afraid that they would kill him as they did his mother a year earlier.

The doctor was distraught because he left them there and he did not tell the nurse to put them out. We spoke for an hour. I informed the coroner that I would obtain an autopsy of Donald's body. I visited Donald's grave to identify it to order a headstone. I returned to verify that the headstone had been set on the correct site. When I returned to the coroner's office to order the autopsy, that office called the cemetery to confirm if Donald's body was there. A young woman informed the coroner's office that Donald's body had been moved by his brother Terry to another burial site. They did not know what cemetery his body was moved to because Terry picked the body up in a limousine. I immediately went back to this cemetery and was informed that my headstone was left behind. I went to the grave site and noticed that the headstone had sunk approximately eighteen inches. Donald's casket clearly was not sitting under his headstone. At that moment, I knew that the autopsy would never happen. I went to the police in that parish and was told that there was nothing I could do.

This feeling going through me could not be contained. I cried for two years. I homeschooled my grandson and continued working as a nurse. But until I dreamed that Donald visited me and talked to me concerning my mission in Africa, I wasn't able to function without grieving. The song "It's been a long time coming but I know that a change is about to come" came to me after that experience.

Three years later, I twisted my ankle when I stepped on a broken water meter cover in 1999. I prayed to Father God to direct me to an honest attorney. I checked the yellow pages and spiritually chose Josiah Eon. I called this attorney's office and set a date for his representation injury. He agreed to represent me against the City of New Orleans Sewage and Water Board. I talked to Josiah Eon concerning my travel to Africa. He informed me that he was from Cameroon, Africa, and planned to return with his mother in a few months. I explained to Attorney Josiah Eon that this trip is for me to set up a business that would bring black youths home to help them stop shooting each other and gain pride in themselves. I informed Josiah Eon that my grandson Arthur Jr. would be travelling with me. He asked me to return in one week and he would have information on what Arthur Jr., and I needed to do in preparation for the trip. I followed these directions, and I obtained for Arthur Jr. his passport from Immigration. I had obtained my passport two years earlier. Arthur Jr. and I reported to the City of New Orleans Health Department to receive the vaccinations we needed. I received a settlement from the City of New Orleans for the ankle injury and purchased for Arthur Jr. and me roundtrip plane tickets to Cameroon, Africa. Arthur Jr. was nine years old when he first visited Africa. The plane trip was interesting in that we had to travel to Europe first in Air France. We waited several hours in an East African country before we proceeded to Cameroon, Africa. We arrived in Cameroon at 9:15 p.m., and we were met by Daniel, Josiah Eon's first cousin. Daniel asked Arthur Jr. and me to call him Daniel. He had hired two taxi drivers for all of us. Josiah Eon and his mother loaded their belongings in a different taxi. Daniel joined Arthur Jr. and me, instructing our taxi driver to a hotel in the city of Douala.

After checking into the hotel, Josiah Eon and his mother proceeded to a family home in the mountains of Limbe, Cameroon, with a promise of seeing Arthur and me for breakfast. The hotel was low budget, and I immediately sprayed the mattress, headboard, and footboard with Raid. Yes, I did smuggle Raid into Africa. Arthur Jr. went to sleep, but I stayed awake because Shango was speaking to me through his lightning bolts and Aggua (Mount Cameroon) was welcoming me through the volcano's rumblings. I sat on the window seat and watched the lightning dance across the sky all night. Actually, this was the first time I communicated with Shango for several hours. This was the first time I communicated with Aggua ever because I don't remember being this close to a volcano erupting.

Seven o'clock the following morning, Daniel knocked on our hotel room door, and he was surprised that I had recognized and understood what the angels were saying to me. He had no idea that the volcano was erupting. He stated that he heard nothing during the night, and no one informed him that the volcano was rumbling. Daniel, Arthur Jr., and I went to breakfast in a sidewalk restaurant. We ordered grits, bacon, eggs, and biscuits with butter and strawberry jam and orange juice. The price was under three dollars for all three of us. Coffee was not ordered but was available if desired. Breakfast was delicious and filling. We walked around for the entire day, only resting for a soda or lemonade. Doula, Cameroon, is a city filled with hundreds of tribes from different countries in Africa. We blend in because we resembled one of the many tribes living in Cameroon, Africa. Several days found Arthur and me visiting ministers in South Cameroon who became interested in my business proposal. On the eighth day, Daniel, Arthur, and I traveled to the northern half of Cameroon to visit Josiah Eon's and Daniel's families. The leaders of their village invited me to lunch. We arrived in the village of Mamfre the next day. We checked into a hotel that was filled with white Americans who were eloquent. These people met at this hotel to discuss any problem and to display how their lives were enriched. They live in Mount Cameroon which was very surprising to me. One couple was originally from New Orleans and had raised two boys here. I was informed by them that they are never returning to the United States. I thought that I would see them again, but that did not happen. This event was surprising; however, it gave me a view of life that was life changing.

Daniel arrived and we preceded to Josiah Eon's mother's home where she prepared dinner for us. There were twelve men sitting at an oval table in the dinner room. When I walked in with Arthur, everyone stood and kissed my right hand and shook Arthur's right hand. A chair was pulled out from the table for me to sit with them. Josiah Eon was sitting on the sofa playing a game with two little boys. He invited Arthur to sit with him until the men were finished questioning me. Oddly, the questions were concerning who I would marry from their tribe. I told them that I dreamed of Daniel before I ever me him. I explained that God sent me to set up a program whereby African American youths could come to Africa to wake them up whereby these young people can see where they come from. My theory is that if you know who you are, you won't kill or steal from your brothers. These young people will know that they are somebody and their lives matter. I did not know that Father God had another plan that merged with my marriage to Daniel. We enjoyed our time with the leaders and went back to the hotel where we slept all night. The following morning, the three of us walked around the village and we came upon an old rope bridge.

Daniel explained to me and Arthur Jr. that the rope bridge was over a hundred years old. The elders of his village forbid them to walk across the bridge. He informed us that the bridge ended at a cave that his people blocked with huge boulders from the mountain above the cave.

I confessed to Daniel that I dreamt of this rope bridge the night before. My vision showed me walking across this bridge focusing on the person at the other end. I could see that a naked, light-skinned young black male was in the fetal position. While trying to recognize the person, twins appeared, took a hand on each side of me, and walked with me. Three-fourths of the trip, the twins ran ahead of me and explained to me that I could not come all the way with them. They told me that the young man was my fourth son, and he was not crossing back with them. They explained that he was confused and angry. I cried on that bridge but continued to move forward with the twins' assistance. I was able to talk to my son and asked him to go into the light. My brother Donald appeared and placed a white robe on his nephew. He smiled, facing the twins, and nodded to me. My son smiled and telepathically told me that he was sorry for everything he did to me and that he would make it up on the other side. He turned and walked into the cave that had boulders closing it. My twins ran to my side and hugged me tightly saying, "Our work here is finished." We walked back to Daniel and Arthur Jr. My twins allowed me to see them. Neither Arthur Jr. nor Daniel could see the twins. I had not conceived the twins yet.

The next day, Daniel's oldest brother Eli appeared at the hotel to bring Arthur Jr. and me to the airport to return home to America. Eli and Arthur Jr. took a walk while Daniel and I had a sexually romantic thirty minutes. Daniel had a very difficult time allowing me to go. He was allowed to walk Arthur Jr. and me to the waiting area. He pointed to hundreds of people who had come to wish me a safe trip back to America and encouraged me to return. I had never in my life felt the love I felt at that moment.

These strangers knew who I am and my mission in this life. It made me feel complete and that my mission here in Africa was in tune with my Father God's will. "Never Had a Love Like This Before."

Once home, I concentrated on returning to Cameroon to marry Daniel and start operating the business IFA-My Brothers' Keeper-Shangobi Bi. Arthur Jr. and I returned to Cameroon, Africa in August 2001. We were there for a month, and I visited the sick and laid hands on them for healing. With one lady, I remember the opposite happening. Usually, I take the negative energy from them, not knowing how to expel it for days. However, this lady had AIDS. I did not hesitate to lay hands on her with the Holy Spirit flowing through me into her. This was the first time that the energy flowed from me into the person I was praying for. Daniel and I was married the next day. We celebrated for several days and were blessed by many. I was successful in obtaining support from several chiefs and ministers.

Soon after, Arthur Jr. and I returned to America. I knew that I was pregnant with twins. Daniel was worried that he may lose me and the twins. The medicine man in Daniel's village talked to Daniel and me at great length. He told me to do nothing while carrying the infants. I could walk for exercise but no housework or laundry. When I became five-month gestation, I went to my family doctor. He monitored me twice a week. He made an appointment with a radiologist for an MRI and ultrasounds. When I received the films, I could see the perfectly formed twins. My family doctor instructed me on the dangers of ectopic pregnancy. He told me that the twins would not pass through my womb because it had been removed years earlier. I convinced him that I could carry the twins to full term. When I reached nine months, I went into labor. I was admitted to Temple Hospital Emergency Room on June 19, 2002. The emergency room physician examined me, and I gave him my ultrasounds and MRI films of my pregnancy. He looked over the films and ordered the radiology department to take more MRIs and ultrasound films. This emergency room doctor claims that he consulted with a surgeon, but the nursing staff informed me that they were ordered not to touch me. No vital signs, no monitoring contractions, no entering my room. I verbally complained to the nurse assigned to me and the nurse supervisor assigned to that floor. Arthur Jr. spent the night of June 19, 2002, with me. He slept on a chair that reclined to a single bed. I had Arthur Jr. go home with a childhood friend, Hope, on June 20, 2002. He spent the night at her home and returned the following morning on June 21, 2002. All day June 20, 2002, and June 21, 2002, the hospital staff attempted to contact the surgeon who had accepted my case. The emergency room doctor who consulted with him was off on June 20, 2002, and the hospital could not contact him.

Dr. Jerry Steven came to my hospital room at seven in the evening of June 21, 2002. Dr. Jerry Steven explained to me that he never spoke to the emergency room physician. The emergency room physician spoke to his answering service who reached his that evening late. He stated to me that he scheduled me for surgery at two the following morning. My question was, how can he schedule me for surgery if he hasn't seen the radiologist's report or films? However, my guardian angel whispered not to question him, and I did not. I was in so much pain that he was walking out of my room when I called out to him that I needed to get the contrast out of my intestine because the radiology films were ordered with contrast. He asked me how I understood so much. That's when Dr. Jerry Steven was informed that I was a nurse. He rushed out of my room. I could not sleep, so I talked with Arthur Jr. He was so afraid that he would lose me. I had him lie down next to me, and we prayed together. Arthur Jr. was asleep when I was taken to the surgery suite just after midnight that night. A nurse for the 11 p.m. – 7 a.m. shift was a friend from nursing school, Violet Keys. She expressed to me that she was very concerned because my surgeon was responsible for a Black American woman and her baby's death two weeks earlier. She and I prayed before the orderly came to deliver me to the surgery suite.

The nurses prepared me for surgery by inserting needles for normal saline and other medicines needed. The anesthetists came into the surgery suite to attain information to ensure that I was the patient who should be there and that I knew why I was having the surgery. I recognized him and his nurse from another hospital I worked through the nursing agency. The last question he asked was, "Are you pregnant?"

I answered, "Yes, I am pregnant. And I have been in labor since June 18, 2002, right here in this hospital. Please look at the MRI and ultrasound film lite-up on the wall to your left." Dr. Jerry Steven walked into the surgery room and escorted the anesthetist out of the room to talk to him. The anesthetist's nurse knew me and promised me that I would receive my twins after this surgery to remove them. Dr. Jerry Steven did not come to my room until June 22, 2002. I asked for a laxative because the surgery was performed with the contrast in my intestines. He explained to me that my twins died in surgery. Several nurses came to my room later to inform me that the camera on the emergency ramp shows two incubators being loaded into an ambulance an hour after the babies were born.

Dr. Steven came back several hours later to change his statement to "You were not pregnant, and I removed copious amount of scar tissue." I asked him to leave my room. I called the lab to be informed that no specimen was presented to them from Dr. Jerry Steven. A white male nurse came into my room with a needle filled with a cloudy white liquid saying that Dr. Jerry Steven ordered the injection. I enlightened him to the fact that I have been a nurse since 1982 and I mostly worked the emergency room and ICU. He returned later with a notepad and asked me what names I wanted on the birth record application. I gave him Daniel Takang Jr. for the boy and Myra Takang for the girl. He left my room, and I never saw him again. A female nurse entered my room to discharge me, but she left and didn't return. I called the nurses' supervisor, and she allowed me to sign myself out. My son Arthur appeared, and he wanted to force the nurses to find the twins. I begged him to get us out of the facility. We got out of the hospital safely because we did not exit where most people enter or exit. When Arthur turned his car on Gen. Taylor Street, we saw two black males standing against the hospital wall with guns in handwriting for someone to come out of the hospital through the emergency room exit.

We escaped unharmed, and my oldest son Arthur Sr. safely assisted me up a flight of stairs to my apartment. The very next day, I received a call from the radiology department asking if I wanted the MRI and ultrasounds films. I informed the clerk that I would be there in an hour. I went to the FBI office to submit some of these films taken at Temple Hospital hours after my admission. The films clearly showed twins in a standing position. I also contacted PAC television, Aaron "The Ballet or the Bullet" Lewison "My Story." According to the FBI, Temple Hospital and Dr. Jerry Steven was under investigation through them since 1992-ten years-for complains from black females that their babies were murdered in the womb or immediately after birth, and not one of these infants' bodies was given to the mothers although many asked for their babies' bodies. How can there be evidence that this was occurring but was never reported to the public? My babies were born in June 2002. How many doctors, hospitals, and agencies are committing genocide on black infants and hiding behind the law? *Roe v. Wade*, 410 USs 113 (1973), is a landmark decision by the United States Supreme Court. In general, it makes abortions up to three months pregnancy legal. In my case, the Supreme Court of the United States of America allowed this doctor and hospital to get away with murder because I was nine months pregnant. An agency, Planned Parenthood, was accused of giving abortions to their clients and selling the aborted infants body parts. This agency confessed on national television that they made money from the infants' aborted body parts to supplement the funds they received through state and federal grants. Dr. Jerry Steven lost his medical license several times just in New Orleans, Louisiana. He was reinstated without losing much time from surgery or killing black infants for body parts. I went to the Medical Review Panel in 2004 and received a report that listed dates of reinstatement and no written reports or details. I was informed by the clerk for the Medical Review Panel that this organization could not give me any information and the site was not available to the public, only attorneys.

I filed a federal lawsuit in the Fifth District Court in New Orleans, Louisiana, and was informed that I had to file the case in the state court. I was instructed to return if I was not satisfied with the results in the state court by the federal judge. I filed a complaint to the Medical Review Panel against Dr. Jerry Steven in 2004. This is the information I received from them in 2015. This information can be obtained from the internet today.

Multiple documents are available.

Type	Date	Description
Board Order	6/25/2012	STEVEN, Jerry, M.D. Order Susp 6-25-12.pdf
Board Order	1/26/2011	STEVEN, Jerry, M.D. Reinstate P 1-26-11.pdf
Consent Order	9/20/2010	STEVEN, Jerry, M.D. Supr Consent Order 9-20-10.pdf
Consent Order	2/19/2010	STEVEN, Jerry, M.D. Susp 2-19-10.pdf
Board Order	5/30/2006	STEVEN, Jerry, M.D. Reinstate on Probation 5-30-06.pdf
Consent Order	9/22/2004	STEVEN, Jerry, M.D. Consent 9-22-04.pdf
Board Order	6/20/2001	STEVEN, Jerry, M.D. Reinstate 6-20-01.pdf
Consent Order	1/25/1996	STEVEN, Jerry, M.D. Consent 1-25-96.pdf
Board Order	11/12/1992	STEVEN, Jerry, M.D. Suppl Order 11-12-92.pdf
Decision	7/16/1992	STEVEN, Jerry, M.D. Decision 7-16-92.pdf

I was informed that this information can be obtained on the internet today. I attempted to enter these evidences into the Fifth District Court; but the clerk, Ms. Bonnie, refused to take the motion saying, "The judge must ask for evidence." Actually Ms. Bonnie refused my motion to enter evidence on several occasions. When I received a court order on November 30, 2015, between then thirty and eleven in the morning during a scheduling conference, I was happy. This conference allowed the defendants to state that they objected to plaintiff entering evidence. Actually, I went from the Court of Appeals in New Orleans to the building across the street to obtain the detailed information above on February 2, 2015. This case has showed me how corrupt our federal and state jurisdictional system have become. The Fifth District Court dismissed my case and had not dismissed all the defendants, so the Fifth Circuit Court of Appeals sent the case back to the Fifth District Court. I was mailed a scheduling conference notice by the court case manager, Jack Hill. The attorney for defendant Children and Family Services was not present, and I questioned Mr. Hill concerning their truant. Mr. Hill explained that Children and Family Services dismissal was over a year, and they would not be involved in this process. The attorneys for James Montgomery, CEO for Temple Hospital, and Dr. Jerry Steven objected during this conference call to me entering evidence. Actually, he was not given a date with the two weeks I was ordered to submit the disclosure requirements of FRCP 26(a)(1). 26(f), and Local Rule 26 and the corporate disclosure requirements of FRCP 7.1. I compiled with the order from the court and submitted to the defendants, the mandatory initial disclosures. I informed Mr. Hill and the attorney(s) for Temple Hospital and James Montgomery that I would be submitting the disclosure requirements of FRCP 26(a)(1), 26(f), and Local Rule 26 and the corporate disclosure requirement of FRCP 7.1 as soon as I was permitted to do so. I supplied the defendants under the discovery disclosure requirements of FRCP 26(a)(1), 26(f), and Local Rule 26 and the corporate disclosure requirement of FRCP 7.1.

The judge, upon hearing from the attorneys for the defendants, dismissed my case again from the Fifth District Court. The undisputed evidence has been submitted under the court rules, and I am now in the Fifth Circuit Court of Appeals waiting for justice. I have contracted the state agency Children and Family Services and submitted the discovery disclosure requirements of FRCP 26(a)(1), 26(f), and Local Rule 26 and the corporate disclosure requirement of FRCP 7.1.

President Obama called a news conference and stated that he was coming to New Orleans in June 2016 to investigate why a woman's, who was fighting for her twins, constitutional rights have been violated. It is now October 4, 2016, and the Fifth Circuit Court of Appeals has agreed with the lower court. My case was dismissed by the Court of Appeals. I felt weak and worn, so I sang this song morning, noon, and night.

"Precious Lord take my hand lead me on help me stand. I am tired, I am weak, and I am worn. Through the dark, through the light lead me on to the light take my hand precious Lord and lead me on."

The Supreme Court of the United States was my final goal to receive my twins; and all I had to write the Petition for Writ of Certiorari to the Supreme Court was me, myself, and Father GOD. This was difficult because I am now talking about the lower courts' inability to allow my complaint into the federal court arena although my constitutional rights have clearly been violated by the defendants.

One thing that's obvious in my journey are the surgeries I absolutely needed, which happened when I had to submit written documents to the courts. When Children and Family Services requested the case to be dismissed, there were bone fragments moving into my right eye socket, and I had to have emergency surgery two weeks before I had to respond to the motion to dismiss the complaint against Children and Family Services. Although I had proof and attempted to enter it as evidence to prevent my case from being dismissed, Ms. Bonnie, pro se clerk for the Fifth Circuit Court of Eastern District, refused to accept it. Here we are, and I fell and tore my right rotator cuff six days before the Fifth Circuit Court of Appeals dismissed my case in agreement with the lower court. Now I must write the Petition for Writ of Certiorari to the Supreme Court with a sling on my right arm, and it is to be removed only when I shower or bath. I prayed and typed for ten days. I mailed the Writ of Certiorari to the Supreme Court on November 14, 2016, and I received approval and my docket number on the 16th of November 2016. Now we wait for the defense attorneys to answer by December 16, 2016, my birthday!

I received the answer from Louisiana Children and Family Services, and their answer is no contest to my charges. It was mailed to me on the form that the Supreme Court requested back in a timely manner. However, counsels for Temple Hospital and Dr. Jerry Steven answered me eight days late with a document not requested by the court stating, "timelessness to be the problem."

My birthday was on the Supreme Court date. I got through to the court several days later and was informed that a conference day will be set. I sit here before my computer amazed that every year now, I pray for my twins to rejoin me and meet their father and other family members. If the Justices in the Supreme Court of the United States are just, it is about to happen.

Today is Christmas 2016, and I am alone because of the gag order again. I clicked and my younger sister and brother brought me back to mother earth a few days earlier. How am I contending with this? Father God and my relationship with him are forever and forever. Amen.

I was successful because I don't have fear and the love I have for my Father God is too high and too deep for anyone to describe it, let alone stop it. I was instructed by my friends and spiritual mentors to prepare to travel to Africa and meet my spiritual husband. Because I listened and obeyed, the mercy of Father God walks with me and sometimes he carries me when life seems to be too much. Thank you, Lord. I just want to thank you, Lord.

My mission had just begun in 2002 when I delivered twins – a boy and a girl. When the twins opened the portal for God's warring angels to come through for ten years, the last angel who came through happened ten years later. Now we wait to reunite and begin our spiritual journey together through my Father's will. It will be done on earth as it is heaven.

The Supreme Court of the United States mailed their decision on my case, and I received it the day after President Donald Trump inauguration. The sentence stated, "Writ of Certiorari denied." When I read the court's rule, I understood that receiving a docket number meant that Writ of Certiorari was granted. I also received two forms that I had to mail to the defendants inquiring if the defendants would be defending my charges. I received the form back from Children and Family Services stating that they would not defend my charges. The attorneys for the hospital and doctor did not mail their form to me but provided a letter form explaining that they had a problem with timelessness. I called the clerk of the Supreme Court of the United States of America and asked what I had to do after receiving this information. The clerk informed me that the head judge had the case and was in fact choosing other judges who would hear the case. I was also informed at that time by the clerk that I would hear from them shortly.

I cried because I felt that I failed the unborn babies that Dr. Steven killed in the wombs of black women from 1998 through 2012, the period when the Medical Review Board stopped receiving complaints from mothers who reported that their babies died in surgery under Dr. Steven.

I'm hurt, angry, and disappointed. I have worked from the day of my twins' birth to the day they were taken by Dr. Jerry Steven out of the hospital. Yes, I'm angry with my government especially the past president of the United States. Hurt, anger, nor disappointment can define what or how I feel. I hold my Father God's love below me, above me, and around me.

God promised never to leave me, and if you believe he speaks to your soul, know that you are a member of the numbers St. John speaks of walking up the king's highway. Will I see my twins one day? Yes. I believe my Father God, for he is not a man that he should lie.

Now is the time for Father God's people to fall on your knees and hear his voice. We as a people did not elect this new president into the presidency, but Father God put him there. Read the Book of Revelation. *Wake up now!*

Everything that has breath, praise ye the Lord.

ABOUT THE AUTHOR

Being born into a highly spiritual family was the perfect place to complete the Father's will. However, there were many who recognized IFA-Kemi from a prophecy spoken hundreds of years before her birth. Few said, "Let God's will be done." Many said, "No, not a female doing his will in my lifetime in this family." However, God's will through IFA-Kemi was completed because she recognized her soul mission. The good, positive energy assisted her through prayers and allowed her to expose the truth on radio, television, and through the judicial system. The bad, negative energy threw everything at her including the kitchen sink. And the ugly, pure, evil, which met her whenever she felt she needed spiritual strength, preceded to block her every move. She never doubted that God held her in the palm of his hands.

Through life experiences, Yoruba obtaining Orumila in Nigeria, Africa, IFA-Kemi and education master's degrees in theology, psychology, hypnotherapy, sociology, public health, and PhD in public health, she continues to assist others on the path of light, seeking to recognize their soul missions.

Love always.
Keep the faith.
Dr. Patricia Peter Takang